Applying the Standards:
Evidence-Based Writing
Grade 5

Credits
Author: Christy Howard
Copy Editor: Julie B. Killian

Visit carsondellosa.com for correlations to Common Core, state, national, and Canadian provincial standards.

Carson-Dellosa Publishing, LLC
PO Box 35665
Greensboro, NC 27425 USA
carsondellosa.com

ISBN 978-1-4838-1457-5
02-215151151

Table of Contents

Introduction

Common Core writing standards focus on three main text types: opinion/argumentative, informative/explanatory, and narrative. A fourth category, research writing, is essential to any evidence-based writing program.

Research shows that effective writing strategies include every step of the writing process: prewriting/brainstorming, drafting, revising, editing/proofreading, and publishing. Students will be walked through these steps on pages 6–10. The Writing Practice Packet can be reused for additional practice by changing the topic.

The writing exercises in this book are designed to go beyond basic writing conventions. Students will learn how to base opinions on evidence, infer facts from relevant details, convey accurate background information, and recount real or imagined experiences. Students' critical thinking skills are engaged when they do research, consider and analyze information, and respond to writing prompts. Writing prompts are paired with graphic organizers and followed by thinking/writing challenges.

Common Core Alignment Chart

Use this chart to plan instruction, practice, or remediation of a standard.

Common Core State Standards*		Practice Pages
Writing Standards		
Text Types and Purposes	5.W.1–5.W.3	11–63
Production and Distribution of Writing	5.W.4–5.W.6	11–63
Research to Build and Present Knowledge	5.W.7–5.W.9	11, 13, 17–36, 40, 42, 45–47, 50–63
Range of Writing	5.W.10	Adapt writing prompts to cover this standard.
Language Standards		
Conventions of Standard English	5.L.1–5.L.2	11, 13, 16–18, 20–23, 25, 26, 31–33, 36, 39, 41–43, 47, 49–51, 55, 61–63
Knowledge of Language	5.L.3	12, 14, 15, 19, 28, 34–35, 38, 44
Vocabulary Acquisition and Use	5.L.4–5.L.6	24, 27, 29, 30, 37, 40, 45, 46, 48, 52–54, 56–60

About This Book

Use this book to teach your students to read closely, or to notice words, structure, and points of fact. The writing prompts that begin on page 11 are intended to engage students' interests and then to send them off on a hunt for more information. Graphic organizers will help students organize their thoughts and research notes. Their actual writing will take place on separate sheets of paper. Encourage students to share their writing with peers, teachers, and other adults. Show students how to use the Student Writing Checklist on page 5. Allow time for thoughtful revisions. Publication is an important Common Core component of writing standards; students should be given access to computers, tablets, or copying machines.

Common Core-Aligned Writing Rubric

Use this rubric as a guide to assess students' written work. You may also offer it to students to help them check their work or as a tool to show your scoring.

4	_____ Offers insightful reasoning and strong evidence of critical thinking _____ Responds skillfully to all of the items in the prompt _____ Uses a logical organizational structure, including introductory and concluding sentences or paragraphs _____ Skillfully connects ideas with linking words and phrases _____ Uses vivid dialogue where appropriate _____ Skillfully supports topic(s) and opinions with evidence
3	_____ Offers sufficient reasoning and evidence of critical thinking _____ Responds to all items in the prompt _____ Uses introductory and concluding sentences _____ Connects ideas with appropriate linking words and phrases _____ Uses dialogue where appropriate _____ Supports topic(s) and opinions with evidence
2	_____ Demonstrates some evidence of critical thinking _____ Responds to some items in the prompt _____ Shows some understanding of paragraph formation _____ Connects some ideas with linking words and phrases _____ Uses some dialogue where appropriate _____ Supports topic(s) and opinions with little evidence
1	_____ Demonstrates limited or no evidence of critical thinking _____ Responds to some or no items in the prompts _____ Shows little or no understanding of paragraph structure _____ Presents ideas or events in random sequence _____ Uses little or no dialogue where appropriate _____ Topic(s) or opinions are not supported by evidence.

 © Carson-Dellosa · CD-104828 · Applying the Standards: Evidence-Based Writing

Student Writing Checklist

Prewrite/Brainstorm

_____ Consider and choose the topic for your essay.

_____ Research your topic on the Internet, in books, or in magazines.

_____ Take notes.

_____ Summarize what you have learned.

Draft

_____ Organize the essay by topics. Separate topics by paragraphs.

_____ Provide an introduction, a body, and a conclusion in the essay.

_____ Support opinions and points of view with reasons.

_____ Develop the topic with facts and definitions.

_____ Include details to describe thoughts, feelings, or actions.

_____ Show evidence in your writing (*for example, because, The author said, I noticed on page ____, Based on what I read online*).

Revise

_____ Write each sentence with a subject and verb.

_____ Sequence events in the order they occurred.

_____ Make sure sentence meaning is clear.

_____ Use specific nouns, lively verbs, and interesting adjectives.

_____ Use a variety of sentence structures.

Edit/Proofread

_____ Indent each paragraph.

_____ Capitalize the first letter in each sentence.

_____ Capitalize all proper nouns.

_____ Spell all words correctly.

_____ Use proper grammar, including subject/verb agreement.

_____ Use proper punctuation, including quotation marks.

Publish

_____ Make sure your final copy is neat—no wrinkles, creases, or holes.

_____ Erase any smudges or dirty spots.

_____ Use good spacing between words.

_____ Use your best handwriting or typing.

_____ Include illustration(s) if appropriate.

Step 1: Prewrite/Brainstorm

Think about, plan, and organize your writing. Use the Internet, books, or magazines to find new information about your topic. Take notes.

Idea 1

Choose a topic

Best Place to Vacation

Idea 2

Idea 3

Idea 4

My choice

Reason 1

Fact/Example

Reason 2

Fact/Example

Reason 3

Fact/Example

Conclusion

Step 2: Draft

Use the information from the organizer on page 6. Write a report about your topic. Remember to support your reasons with facts and details. Use linking words or phrases such as *in addition* and *specifically*. Separate your ideas into paragraphs. In your conclusion, restate your opinion.

_____

_____

_____

_____

_____

_____

_____

_____

_____

_____

_____

_____

_____

_____

_____

_____

_____

_____

_____

_____

Step 3: Revise

Read your essay. Then, answer the questions with *Y* for *yes* or *N* for *no*.

_____ Did I start my story with an interesting introduction that will make readers want to read more?

_____ Did I provide facts and details to support my reasons?

_____ Did I use words such as *in addition* and *specifically* to link my reasons with my opinion?

_____ Are all of my sentences about the topic?

_____ Should I add more details?

_____ Did I break the essay into paragraphs?

_____ Have I used exciting verbs?

_____ Have I used interesting adjectives?

_____ Have I used a variety of sentence structures?

_____ Does my conclusion provide a good ending for the essay by restating my opinion?

The best part of this essay is ...	The part that needs work is ...

Step 4: Edit/Proofread

Place a check mark before each item when you have checked your work.

My Story

_____ I have read my essay, and it makes sense.
_____ It has a beginning, middle, and end.
_____ I stayed on topic.
_____ My sentences are easy for readers to understand.
_____ I used a variety of words.

Capitalization

_____ Each sentence begins with a capital letter.
_____ All proper nouns begin with capital letters.
_____ My title words, except for articles and prepositions, are capitalized.

Punctuation

_____ Each sentence ends with the correct ending punctuation.
_____ I have placed commas where they belong.
_____ I have used quotation marks to show where speech starts and ends.

Spelling

_____ I have checked to see that all words are spelled correctly.
_____ I have looked up words when needed.

Grammar

_____ My subjects and verbs match.
_____ I have used italics or underlining to indicate titles of works.
_____ I have used conjunctions properly.

Peer or Teacher Editing Checklist

Ask another student or teacher to look at your writing and mark *Yes* or *No*.

Is the first word of each sentence capitalized?	Yes	No
Are the proper nouns capitalized?	Yes	No
Does each sentence end with a punctuation mark?	Yes	No
Are the words spelled correctly?	Yes	No
Are the paragraphs indented?	Yes	No
Is the handwriting or typing easy to read?	Yes	No

Editor's Name _____

Step 5: Publish

When you publish an essay or report, you make it possible for others to read it. Your readers might be teachers, students, or family members.

To publish an impressive essay or report, choose from these options.

1. I choose to publish my writing by

   _____ writing it in neat handwriting.

   _____ typing it on a computer.

   _____ typing it on a tablet.

   _____ copying it on a copier.

2. If I use a cover page, it will include

   _____ the title.

   _____ the author's name.

   _____ the illustrator's name.

   _____ art or illustrations.

3. If appropriate, my presentation will include

   _____ illustration(s) or art.

   _____ captions for the illustration(s) or art.

   _____ a graph, chart, or time line.

4. I will share my writing with

   _____   _____

   _____   _____

Furry Friends

Pets in the classroom can help students learn about animals' lives. Students can learn about the animals' habits and diets. Classroom pets also help students learn responsibility as they care for the animals.

Imagine your teacher has decided to let the class choose a pet for your classroom. Each student will give input for the class vote. What do you think would be a good animal to have as a classroom pet? Brainstorm a list of classroom pets. Choose an animal from the list that you think would make a good classroom pet. Use multiple sources, including the Internet and books, to gather information. Why do you think this animal would be a good choice? Write a letter to your teacher to persuade her to agree with your choice. Provide facts and details to support your opinion.

Prewrite: Use the graphic organizer to brainstorm a list of animals that you think would make good classroom pets. Then, circle your top choice.

Animal choices for a classroom pet	
Introduction	
Reason 1	
Reason 2	
Reason 3	
Conclusion	

☀ Reflect and Revise

1. As you brainstormed your list of potential classroom pets, what animals did you intentionally leave off your list of good classroom pets? Why?

2. Reread your letter. Check for correct capitalization, punctuation, and spelling. Correct any errors.

Name _____

Leader of the Pack

The world has many great leaders. This includes political leaders, school leaders, community leaders, etc. Many leaders have similar characteristics. What does it mean to be a good leader?

Interview adults and classmates. Ask them what it means to be a good leader. Research world, school, or community leaders in books, magazines, or on the Internet. What do these leaders have in common? What are traits you want to see in a leader? Why are these traits important? Write an essay that tells your opinion about traits of good leaders. Use your research and interviews to support your reasoning. After you have finished your first draft, ask an adult to read it and give you feedback. Make any necessary changes.

Prewrite: Use the graphic organizer to record your thoughts.

Good Leader Traits	Why is this trait important?
Trait 1	
Trait 2	
Trait 3	

Reflect and Revise

1. Do you see yourself as a leader? Why or why not? What could you do to be a better leader? What do you do really well as a leader?

2. Reread your essay. Did you include a variety of sentence structures? Revise your essay to make sure you have included simple, compound, and complex sentences.

Meeting of the Minds

Imagine your class has been invited to a leadership luncheon. You will eat lunch and spend time with the head of your country. During this visit, the head of your country wants to hear from you about an important issue that you would like him to address in the upcoming year. Think about an issue in your country that you would like to see fixed.

Brainstorm a list of issues such as homelessness, education reform, joblessness, etc. Choose one issue from the list that you would like to learn more about. Interview adults and classmates to learn their views on the topic. Cite your sources. Why is this issue important to you? Why is it important to others? Write a letter to the head of your country about why you believe he should work to fix this issue. After you have finished your first draft, ask an adult to read it and give you feedback. Make any necessary changes.

Prewrite: Use the graphic organizer to record your thoughts.

Issue	Why is this issue important to you?	Why is this issue important to others?

☀ Reflect and Revise

1. What are possible solutions to the issue you wrote about in your letter? How will these solutions help others?

2. Reread your letter. Check for correct capitalization, punctuation, and spelling. Correct any errors.

One Book

Many schools participate in the *One School, One Book* initiative. Students and teachers in each school read the same book. They share ideas about the characters, events, and themes. This initiative has been known to motivate students to read. It can also build communities of learners. Imagine your school will begin this initiative.

Use the Internet to research the top 25 best-selling or award-winning books for children. Based on your research, which book would you want your school to read? Why did you choose this book? How will this book benefit others? What do you hope they will learn? Write a letter to your principal about your book selection. Give reasons why you think this book would be a good choice for your school.

Prewrite: Use the graphic organizer to plan your letter.

Introduction	
Reason 1	
Reason 2	
Reason 3	
Conclusion	

☀ Reflect and Revise

1. One of the goals of the *One School, One Book* initiative is to build a sense of community within schools. What are some alternative activities your school could do to build a sense of community within your school?

2. Reread your letter. Remember that your audience is your school principal. Have you used formal language and sentence structure to convey your message? If not, consider how you could adjust your word choices to properly address your audience.

Good Health Choices

Many school programs focus on helping students get healthy. Many young children are considered "out of shape." These programs hope to raise awareness about the importance of physical health. They encourage students to eat healthfully and to exercise.

Imagine your school will require all students to exercise in PE classes for 30 minutes each day. Research the benefits of daily exercise in books or on the Internet. Decide if you agree or disagree with the school's requirement. Interview adults and classmates to learn their views on the topic. Write an essay that tells your opinion. Use facts and details to support your reasoning. After you have finished your first draft, ask an adult to read it and give you feedback. Make any necessary changes. Type your final copy.

Prewrite: Use the graphic organizer to record your thoughts.

PE Every Day	
Agree	Disagree

Reflect and Revise

1. It is important that children work to embrace healthful eating and living habits. What are some other ideas you can think of that might help promote more healthful lifestyles for children?

2. Reread your essay. Did you include a variety of sentence structures? Revise your essay to make sure you have included simple, compound, and complex sentences.

Name _____

Making a Change

Each year, schools hope to improve from the previous year. Schools work together to decide how to spend money to meet their goals. Sometimes, this takes the shape of new programs, new technology, or new equipment.

Imagine the principal of your school has asked for students' input about this year's improvements. The school has received a $50,000 award to improve the school. Write a letter to your principal to explain how you think the money should be spent. Interview classmates, teachers, librarians, etc., to learn their views on the topic. Include data from your interviews, as well as your knowledge of the school, in your letter. Use facts and details to support your reasoning.

Prewrite: Use the graphic organizer to plan your letter.

My Opinion	
Introduction	
Reason 1	
Reason 2	
Reason 3	
Conclusion	

Reflect and Revise

1. If you had an unlimited amount of money, what would you change about your school? How would these changes make your school better?

2. Reread your letter. Check for correct capitalization, punctuation, and spelling. Correct any errors.

Voting Rights

Every four years, Americans vote for a president. Voting rights have changed over the years. People have fought to have the right to vote. In the United States, citizens 18 years and older have the right to vote, but this has not always been the case.

Imagine the voting laws will change. Instead of being an *option*, it is now a *requirement* for all American citizens over the age of 18 to vote. Research the women's suffrage movement. Learn more about the history of voting rights for African Americans from books or on the Internet. Interview adults to learn their views on the topic. Write an essay to tell whether you agree or disagree with this new law and why. Use facts and details to support your reasoning.

Prewrite: Use the graphic organizer to plan your essay.

Voting as a Requirement	
I agree because . . .	I disagree because . . .

☀ Reflect and Revise

1. Why is it important to vote? Do you think 18 years old is a good age to be able to vote? Why or why not?

2. Reread your essay. Have you used verb tenses correctly? Are there any inappropriate shifts in verb tense? If so, make any necessary corrections.

Bringing Home the Gold

In 1996, the Summer Olympics were held in Atlanta, Georgia. The Olympics bring people together from around the world to compete in sporting events.

Imagine your hometown may be the location of the next Olympics. Would you want the Olympics to be held where you live? Why or why not? What are the benefits? What are the challenges? Interview people in your community to learn their views on the topic. Write an editorial to tell whether you agree or disagree with the Olympics being held in your hometown. Include data from your interviews, as well as what you know about the Olympics, in your editorial. Use facts and details to support your reasoning.

Prewrite: Use the graphic organizer to write the reasons why you might agree and disagree with the Olympics coming to your hometown.

The Olympics in Your Hometown	
Agree	Disagree

⛭ Reflect and Revise

1. What are the benefits of having Olympic games? What are the benefits of having Olympic games in different places around the world?

2. Reread your editorial. Check for correct capitalization, punctuation, and spelling. Correct any errors.

Weekend TV

Many parents wonder if their children watch too much TV. Many are concerned that some TV programs are too violent. However, some people think watching TV can be educational for children. What do you think?

What if your parents decided you could only watch TV on the weekends? Do you agree or disagree with this? Research the benefits of watching TV on the Internet. Interview classmates and adults to learn their views on the topic. What are the problems with watching too much TV? Write a letter to your parents. Explain why you agree or disagree with their decision. Use facts and details to support your reasoning.

Prewrite: Use the graphic organizer to record your thoughts about why you might agree or disagree with your new TV schedule. Record the benefits of TV watching and the problems with too much of it.

TV Watching	
Agree	Disagree
Benefits of TV watching	Problems with too much TV watching

☀ Reflect and Revise

1. What are some alternative fun educational activities children can do instead of watching TV?

2. Reread your letter. Did you include a variety of sentence structures? Revise your letter to make sure you have included simple, compound, and complex sentences.

Name _____

Freedom for All

The Statue of Liberty is a national monument in New York City. France gave the statue to the United States in 1885. It was dedicated in 1886. The statue represents freedom.

Research ways people have fought to have freedom around the world in books or on the Internet. What freedoms do you have? Do you think everyone should have the same freedoms? Interview adults to learn what freedom means to them. Cite your sources. Write a paper based on your research and interviews to describe what freedom means to you. Use facts and details to support your reasoning.

Prewrite: Use the graphic organizer to record your thoughts and findings.

In what ways have people fought to have freedom?	What freedoms do you have?	Interviews: What does freedom mean?	My thoughts: What does freedom mean to me?

Reflect and Revise

1. The Statue of Liberty is one symbol of freedom. What are some other symbols that represent freedom?

2. Reread your paper. Check for correct capitalization, punctuation, and spelling. Correct any errors.

What about Caffeine?

Caffeine is in many foods and beverages, including tea, soft drinks, and candy. The subject of whether caffeine can cause harm to children has been long debated.

Research the benefits and drawbacks of consuming caffeine in books or on the Internet. Cite your sources. After you have conducted your research, decide if you think children should be allowed to consume foods and beverages that contain caffeine. Why or why not? Write an editorial that tells your opinion. After you have finished your first draft, ask a classmate and an adult to read it and give you feedback. Make any necessary changes.

Prewrite: Use the graphic organizer to record your thoughts and findings.

Caffeine Consumption in Children	
Benefits	Drawbacks

✺ Reflect and Revise

1. Since caffeine may boost energy levels, what are some alternatives to foods and beverages with caffeine? What are some other ways to increase energy levels?

2. Reread your editorial. Check for correct capitalization, punctuation, and spelling. Correct any errors.

More Time to Learn

Over the years, many school districts have debated about how much time students should spend in school. On one hand, some people think the school day should be extended to give students more time for learning. On the other hand, some people think an extended school day would give students less time to participate in sports or other fun activities.

What are your thoughts? Research the pros and cons of extending the school day. Use multiple sources, including books and the Internet, to gather information. Talk to teachers and classmates about their views on the topic. Write a paper to tell what you think about the topic. Tell whether you agree or disagree and why. Use facts and details to support your reasoning.

Prewrite: Use the graphic organizer to record your thoughts and findings.

Pros	Cons

I _____ with a longer school day.
agree/disagree

Reflect and Revise

1. Besides extending the school day, what are some alternative ways to help students learn more at school?

2. Reread your paper. Check for correct capitalization, punctuation, and spelling. Correct any errors.

Choose a Team

Sports give people the chance to build relationships. Sports also provide health benefits and promote self-discipline.

Imagine your parents tell you that you must be a member of a sports team until you graduate from high school. Do you agree or disagree with your parents' decision? Research the benefits of sports in books, magazines, or on the Internet. Interview classmates and adults that are on sports teams to get their views on the topic. Cite your sources. Write a letter to your parents. Tell them why you agree or disagree with their decision. Include data from your research. Use facts and details to support your reasoning.

Prewrite: Use the graphic organizer to brainstorm why you might agree or disagree with your parents' decision.

Agree	Disagree

☀ Reflect and Revise

1. In what other activities could you participate that would give you some of the same benefits of being on a sports team? Explain your answer.

2. Reread your letter. Have you used verb tenses correctly? Are there any inappropriate shifts in verb tense? If so, make any necessary corrections.

Carnivorous Plants

Carnivorous plants are unique plants that gain nutrients by capturing and digesting insects and animals. The plants capture their food by using their exotic traps. There are many types of carnivorous plants. Each plant has different ways of trapping its food.

Use multiple sources, including the Internet and books, to research two different carnivorous plants and write important facts about them. Cite your sources. Where can these plants be found? What do they look like? How do their traps work? How would you describe their leaves? Write an essay that compares and contrasts the two carnivorous plants. Include facts from your research.

Prewrite: Use the graphic organizer to compare and contrast the different plants. Label each side.

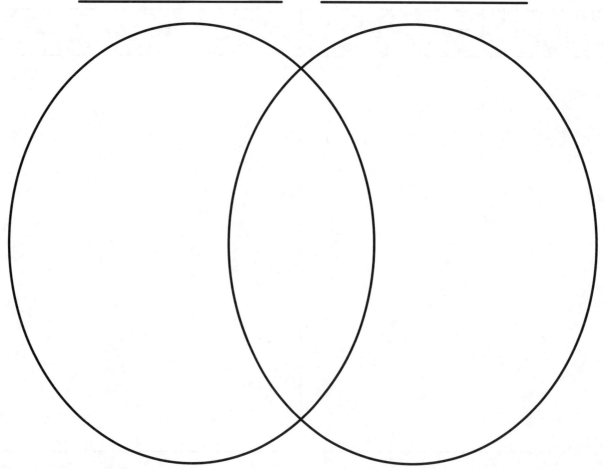

 Reflect and Revise

1. Some insects and animals also trap their food. How are their methods for trapping prey similar to or different from the way plants trap their food?

2. Reread your essay. Have you used grade-appropriate vocabulary and words that signal you are comparing and contrasting the plants? If not, consider your word choices for clarity (for example, *similarly, in contrast, unlike*).

Name _____

History of the Game

James Naismith invented the game of basketball in 1891. Originally, the game was played with a soccer ball. Instead of nets for scoring, peach baskets were used. In 1894, A. G. Spalding's company created the first official basketball. Today, if you look onto a basketball court during a game, you will see five players per team; this is different from how nine players originally made up a team. Things certainly have changed!

Many sports have evolved over time. Choose a sport to research. Use the Internet, magazines, and books to gather information. Cite your sources. Write an essay about the sport and how it may have evolved. After you have finished your first draft, ask an adult to read it and give you feedback. Make any necessary changes. Type your final copy.

Prewrite: Use the graphic organizer to record facts about your chosen sport.

Sport's inventor	
When?	
Where?	
Rules	
Equipment	
How the sport has changed over time	
Other interesting facts about the sport	

Reflect and Revise

1. Sports provide many health benefits for players. What are other benefits of playing sports? Do people who play sports face any challenges? Explain.

2. Reread your essay. Have you used verb tenses correctly? Are there any inappropriate shifts in verb tense? If so, make any necessary corrections.

Take a Hike

More than 140 years ago, the American government protected an area of land that became the first national park in the world. This park is known as Yellowstone National Park. The park allows visitors to engage with nature. Visitors can hike, camp, kayak, etc. Many national parks exist throughout the country and around the world. They focus on nature, culture, and history.

Choose a national park to research. Use the Internet, magazines, and books to gather information. Cite your sources. When was the park created? What are the geographic features? What wildlife lives there? What activities can you do there? Write a report about the park. Include facts from your research. After you have finished your first draft, ask an adult to read it and give you feedback. Make any necessary changes. Type your final copy.

Prewrite: Use the graphic organizer to record facts about your chosen US national park.

Park and Creation Date	Geographic Features	Plants and Wildlife	Activities	Other Interesting Facts

☀ Reflect and Revise

1. Why do you think the world has so many national parks? How are they beneficial?

2. Reread your report. Check for correct capitalization, punctuation, and spelling. Correct any errors.

Name _____

Creepy Crawlers

Many different insects live throughout the world. Often, we find ourselves trying to get away from them because they can literally be a pain! They often leave us with bites and stings. However, some insects benefit people and the environment.

Research to learn which insects benefit people and/or the environment. Choose one insect that you would like to learn more about. Use multiple sources, including the Internet and books, to gather information. Cite your sources. Describe the insect. How does it benefit people? How does it benefit the environment? Write a report about the insect. After you have finished your first draft, ask a classmate or an adult to read it and give you feedback. Make any necessary changes. Type your final copy.

Prewrite: Use the graphic organizer to record facts about how your chosen insect benefits people and the environment.

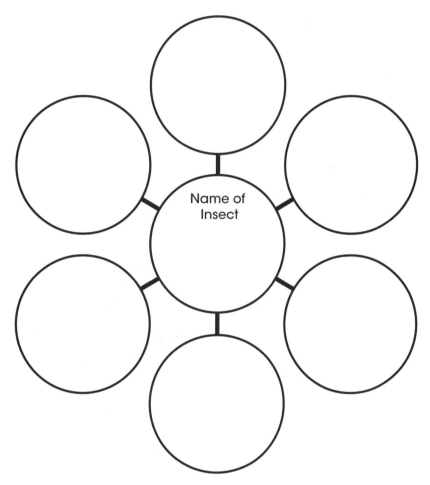

Name of Insect

⚡ Reflect and Revise

1. What would happen if your chosen insect disappeared? How would people be affected? How would the environment be affected?

2. As you researched the insect, did you see words you didn't know? Use context clues to help you understand the words. Use a dictionary if necessary. Use the words and define them in your report.

Name _____

Amazing Authors

Biographies help us learn about the lives of others. Read a biography. How is the biography organized? How does the author of the biography present evidence to the reader? How does she support the evidence? For example, if the author says the person had many achievements, does she tell you about those achievements? Keep this biography in mind as you begin to write a biography about your favorite author.

What are some of your favorite books or stories? Who is your favorite author? Choose an author that you would like to learn more about. Use multiple sources, including the Internet and books, to gather information. Cite your sources. When was this author born? What are the titles of his or her books? What inspires this author to write? Write a biography about this author. After you have finished your first draft, ask a classmate and an adult to read it and give you feedback. Make any necessary changes. Type your final copy.

Prewrite: Use the graphic organizer to record facts about your chosen author.

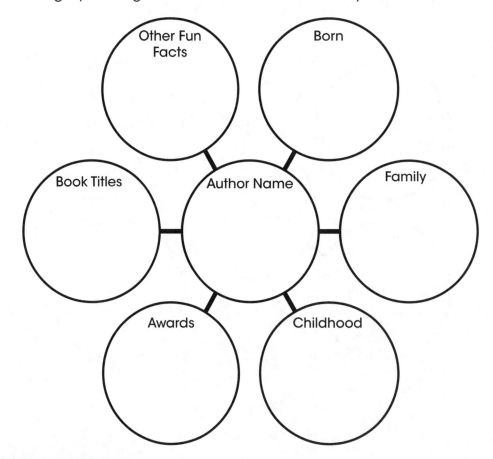

☀ Reflect and Revise

1. Why is this person your favorite author? What do you enjoy most about his or her books?

2. Reread your biography. Did you include a variety of sentence structures? Revise your biography to make sure you have included simple, compound, and complex sentences.

Name _____

Sharing Stories

Many cultures have myths and fairy tales with similar themes. For example, different cultures have many "Cinderella" stories. Different cultures also have many "Little Red Riding Hood" stories. Read the story of "Cinderella" from two different cultures. Compare and contrast the settings, characters, and events. How are the stories the same? How are they different? Are the problems the same? Are they solved the same way? Write an essay to compare and contrast the stories.

Prewrite: Use the graphic organizer to record your findings.

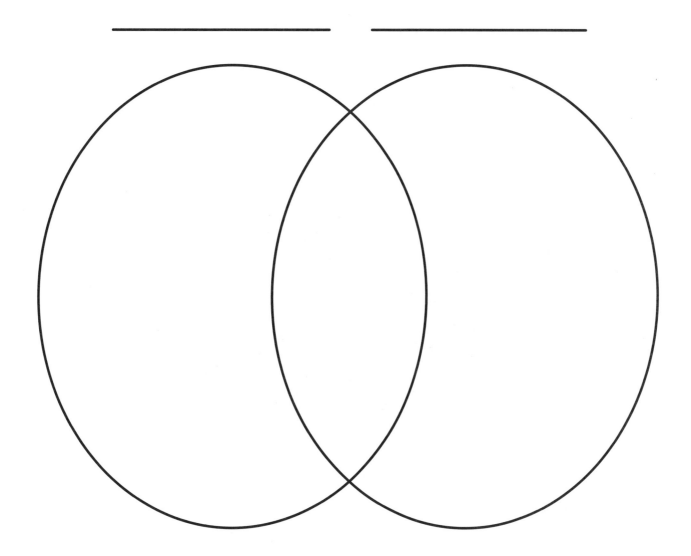

⁂ Reflect and Revise

1. Of the two stories you read, which one did you enjoy the most? Why? What did you learn about the two cultures from reading the two stories?

2. Reread your essay. Have you used grade-appropriate vocabulary and words that signal you are comparing and contrasting the stories? If not, consider your word choices for clarity (for example, *similarly, in contrast, unlike*).

Endangered Species

For many years, endangered species have been protected. Animal protection agencies have worked to support laws that protect animals in danger of extinction.

Choose an endangered species that you would like to learn more about. Use the Internet, magazines, and books to gather information. Where can the species be found? Why is it considered an endangered species? What food does it eat? What other fun facts can you find? Write a report about the species. After you have finished your first draft, ask a classmate and an adult to read it and give you feedback. Make any necessary changes. Type your final copy.

Prewrite: Use the graphic organizer to record facts about your chosen endangered species.

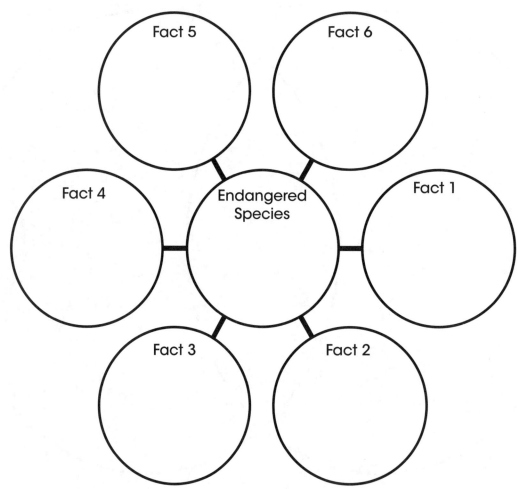

 Reflect and Revise

1. Aside from placing endangered species on a list, what other steps can people take to protect them?

2. As you researched the endangered species, did you see words you didn't know? Use context clues to help you understand the words. Use a dictionary if necessary. Use the words and define them in your report.

Name _____

Women in History

Women have played important roles in world history. They have been pioneers and leaders across the globe. Women around the world have contributed to progress in science, politics, and many other fields.

Choose a famous woman in history that you would like to learn more about. Use multiple sources, including the Internet and books, to gather information. Cite your sources. Who is this woman? What is she known for? What did you learn about her family? Did she face any challenges in life? What were her accomplishments? Write a report about your findings. After you have finished your first draft, ask an adult to read it and give you feedback. Make any necessary changes. Type your final copy.

Prewrite: Use the graphic organizer to record facts about your chosen woman in history.

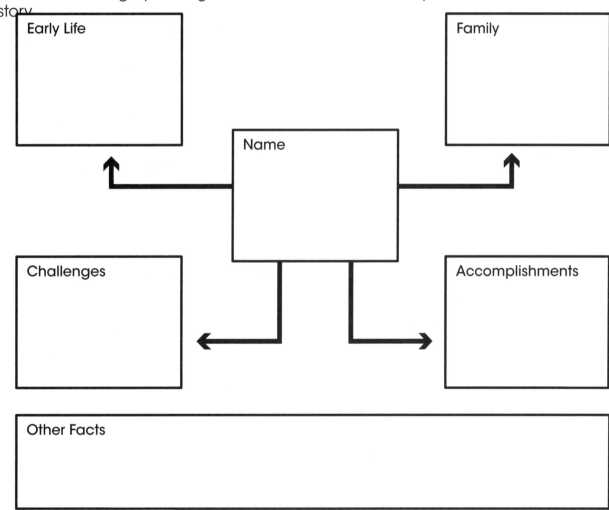

Reflect and Revise

1. Think of a woman you know personally and who positively impacts others' lives. What are some of her character traits? How does she make a positive difference?

2. Reread your report. Have you used verb tenses correctly? Are there any inappropriate shifts in verb tense? If so, make any necessary corrections.

Sea Creatures

Sea horses are fascinating fish. They have many interesting characteristics, including their long heads shaped like those of horses. Sea horses protect themselves by blending in with their environments. They vary in size and are only about the size of jelly beans when they are babies. The male sea horse actually carries the sea horse eggs. When the time comes for the babies to be born, they hatch from a pouch.

The oceans are filled with many intriguing sea creatures. Read about different sea creatures. Choose one sea creature that you would like to learn more about. Use multiple sources, including the Internet and books, to gather information. Cite your sources. Include a picture of the sea creature. What does the sea creature look like? What does it eat? What other facts can you find? Write a report about your findings. Make any necessary changes.

Prewrite: Use the graphic organizer to record facts about your chosen sea creature.

Introduction

Fact 1 _____   Fact 2 _____

Fact 3 _____   Fact 4 _____

Fact 5 _____   Fact 6 _____

Fact 7 _____   Fact 8 _____

Conclusion

Reflect and Revise

1. How does your chosen sea creature interact with other creatures in the ocean? How does it contribute to its habitat? Add any new information to your report.

2. Reread your report. Check for correct capitalization, punctuation, and spelling. Correct any errors.

Name _____

Protecting Our Earth

Earth Day is celebrated each year during the month of April. This day provides an opportunity to celebrate our Earth and focus on protecting our environment. However, we don't have to wait until Earth Day to think about how to keep our Earth healthy.

Research ways you can help protect the environment all year long. What are some things we need to change about our ways of life to help Earth? What organizations work to help us have a clean, healthy Earth? How can you help keep Earth clean? How can you encourage your family members or school to help protect Earth? Use books, magazines, or the Internet to find out more. Write a report to explain ways people can work to protect the environment. Type your final copy.

Prewrite: Use the graphic organizer to record your thoughts and findings.

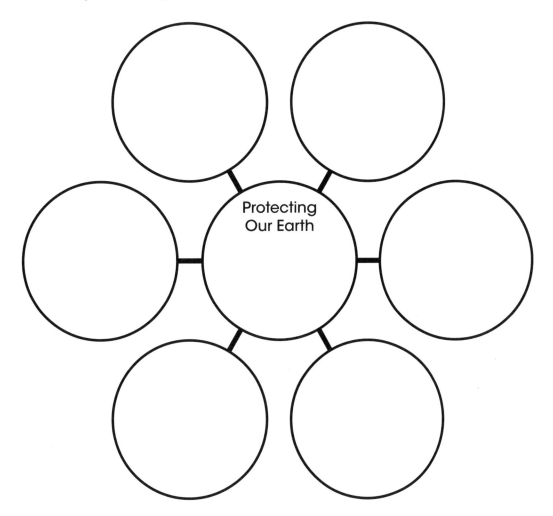

Reflect and Revise

1. Recycling is one way to protect Earth. How can you increase recycling at home and at school?

2. Reread your report. Check for correct capitalization, punctuation, and spelling. Correct any errors.

The Common Cold

Catching colds can be miserable for everyone. Sore throats and runny noses often accompany colds. The common cold can be easily spread through coughing and sneezing. Therefore, it is important to know how to protect yourself from catching a cold.

Research the causes and symptoms of the common cold. Research ways to protect yourself against catching colds. Use the Internet and books to gather information. Cite your sources. Write a report about your findings. After you have finished your first draft, ask a classmate and an adult to read it and give you feedback. Make any necessary changes. Type your final copy.

Prewrite: Use the graphic organizer to record facts about the common cold.

Symptoms	
Causes	
Prevention	

Reflect and Revise

1. Although no cure exists for the common cold, what are some things you can do to make yourself more comfortable while you have a cold?

2. Reread your report. Did you include a variety of sentence structures? Revise your report to make sure you have included simple, compound, and complex sentences.

Name _____

Ecosystems

An ecosystem is an area where living and nonliving things interact in a community. The world contains many different ecosystems such as oceans, lakes, ponds, and forests.

Choose an ecosystem that you would like to learn more about. Use the Internet, magazines, and books to gather information. Cite your sources. Include information about the ecosystem's major parts. What living things are found there? What nonliving things are found there? How do they interact with each other? How does the ecosystem benefit people? Write a report about your findings. Create and label a diagram of your ecosystem. After you have finished your first draft, ask an adult to read it and give you feedback. Make any necessary changes. Type your final copy.

Prewrite: Use the graphic organizer to record facts about your chosen ecosystem.

Introduction

Fact 1 _____   Fact 2 _____

Fact 3 _____   Fact 4 _____

Fact 5 _____   Fact 6 _____

Fact 7 _____   Fact 8 _____

Conclusion

Reflect and Revise

1. What role does water play in your chosen ecosystem? What would happen if it did not have water?

2. Reread your report. Did you include a variety of sentence structures? Revise your report to make sure you have included simple, compound, and complex sentences.

Supporting Our Views

School systems have had many debates about school uniforms. Use the Internet to find an article that supports school uniforms. What reasons does the author give for supporting uniforms? What evidence does the author give to support these reasons? Do you agree with the author's point of view about school uniforms? Why or why not? Do you think it is fair that some students have to wear uniforms and others do not? Why or why not? Write a report about the article.

Prewrite: Use the graphic organizer to record your thoughts.

Reasons	Evidence

Reflect and Revise

1. You read an article that supports school uniforms. If someone were to write an article against school uniforms, what do you think some of the author's reasons might be?

2. Reread your report. Check for correct capitalization, punctuation, and spelling. Correct any errors.

Name _____

The First Time...

The first time each of us tries something new is often a memorable experience. Some of us can remember the first time we rode a roller coaster, went to a zoo, or traveled on an airplane. The first day of school each year is a "first" we all have in common. Create a story about an event or activity that you experienced for the first time. Your story can be real or imaginary. Focus on the sequence of events. Use clear details and descriptive language to make readers feel as though they were there. After you have finished your first draft, ask a classmate and an adult to read it and give you feedback. Make any necessary changes.

Prewrite: Use the graphic organizer to brainstorm ideas for your story.

Characters	
Setting	
Sights	
Sounds	
First	
Next	
Then	
Finally	

☀ Reflect and Revise

1. While often the first time we each do something can be exciting, it can also be scary. What advice would you give to a friend who may be afraid to do something for the first time?

2. Reread your story. Have your word choices helped convey your feelings about the event? Do the readers feel as though they were there? If not, consider adding more descriptive language or using figurative language in your descriptions.

Being Brave

In our lives, we see people who show bravery every day. For some people, such as police officers, firefighters, lifeguards, etc., being brave is part of their jobs.

Write about a time you saw someone show bravery. Have you seen a classmate, parent, or teacher show bravery? Have you seen a Good Samaritan at work? Usually, when someone has to be brave, she must solve a problem. What was the problem? How did the person solve it? If you are unable to think of a real situation, write an imaginary story about someone who showed bravery.

Prewrite: Use the graphic organizer to brainstorm ideas for your story.

Person/Character				
Problem				
Solution				
Sequence of Events	1.	2.	3.	4.

Reflect and Revise

1. What are some challenges people might face as they try to exhibit bravery? Can you think of a time when you had to be brave? What challenges did you face?

2. Reread your story. Did you include a variety of sentence structures? Revise your story to make sure you have included simple, compound, and complex sentences.

Name _____

Memories

Many tools are available to record our memories. We have photo albums, videos, memory books, etc. One common way to record our memories is through journal writing.

Write a journal entry that describes your memories of elementary school. What have been your favorite subjects? Who have been your closest friends? What have been some of your favorite school activities? Have you had school plays or field trips? What are some important lessons you have learned?

Prewrite: Use the graphic organizer to brainstorm ideas for your journal entry.

Favorite Memories (classes, field trips, etc.)	
Challenges	
Celebrations	
What lessons have you learned?	
How have you changed?	
Other interesting thoughts or ideas	

Reflect and Revise

1. As you reflect on your years in elementary school, what are you looking forward to about middle school? What do you hope to learn? What makes you excited or nervous?

2. Reread your journal entry. Have you used verb tenses correctly? Are there any inappropriate shifts in verb tense? If so, make any necessary corrections.

Fears

"I can't do it," Fernando said as he stood in line to get on the roaring roller coaster. "There is simply no way I'm getting up there."

"Come on," his friends coaxed him. "Don't be a chicken!"

Fernando's friends had convinced him to come to the carnival to face his fear of roller coasters. Now, he could feel the anxiety in every breath he took, as fear crept into his belly and made itself comfortable in his beating heart. Standing there waiting, he couldn't decide. Would he live up to the name "chicken" his friends had given him?

You just read a story about Fernando's fear. How did the author describe the fear? What kind of figurative language did you notice? How did this language help you understand Fernando's fear?

Write a story about a time you were afraid. Use transitional words to show the sequence of events. Use descriptive and figurative language to convey the emotions in your story. After you have finished your first draft, ask a classmate and an adult to read it and give you feedback. Make any necessary changes. Type your final copy.

Prewrite: Use the graphic organizer to brainstorm ideas for your story.

Characters	
Setting	
Sights	
Sounds	
First	
Next	
Then	
Finally	

Reflect and Revise

1. What would you say to a friend who is afraid to try something new? What advice would you give him?

2. Reread your story. Have your word choices helped convey your feelings about the event? Do the readers feel as though they are there? If not, consider adding more descriptive language or using figurative language in your descriptions.

Name _____

Favorite Places

Nina loved hiding in her closet. It was the only place she could find privacy away from her younger brothers and sisters. Inside her closet, Nina crept around the wooden floors and imagined herself in amazing adventures. She imagined that she was hiding from a scary creature or making friends with a glowing princess. Sometimes, Nina would sneak into her closet to read her favorite books. She would turn on her book light and get lost in the characters as she quietly turned the pages, hoping no one would find her in her private space.

Where is your favorite place? What makes it so special? How does it look, smell, and sound? Write a story about your favorite place and why you enjoy it. Make it descriptive so that the reader can imagine exactly what it's like to be in your favorite place. Include pictures that represent your special place. Type your final copy.

Prewrite: Use the graphic organizer to brainstorm ideas for your story.

Place	What does it look like?	What does it smell like?	What sounds do you hear when you are there?	What do you like to do in your favorite place?

☀ Reflect and Revise

1. Do you touch any objects that are in your special place? What emotions do you feel in your favorite place? Add these sensory images to your story.

2. Reread your story. Have you used verb tenses correctly? Are there any inappropriate shifts in verb tense? If so, make any necessary corrections.

Imaginary Tales

Fairy tales often have characters who face problems and work together with others to solve those problems. Reread some of your favorite fairy tales. Consider how the authors of the fairy tales developed the characters and plots. What problems do the characters face? How do they solve the problems? How would you solve the problems differently if you were in the stories? What are the settings of the stories? Why are the settings important?

Write your own modern-day fairy tale. What is the problem in your story? It can be a silly problem or a serious problem, but characters must solve the problem. Use dialogue to show how your characters speak to each other.

Prewrite: Use the graphic organizer to brainstorm ideas for your story.

Good characters		Evil characters		
Problem(s)		Solution(s)		
Setting				
Sequence of events	1.	2.	3.	4.

⚡ Reflect and Revise

1. Why do you think children have loved certain fairy tales for hundreds of years?

2. Reread your story. Check for correct capitalization, punctuation, and spelling. Correct any errors.

Facing Challenges

Marcus looked at his legs, wondering if they would carry him over the finish line. Today was his first race since he'd broken his leg at the championship track meet last year. He had done well in practice, but today would be different. Today, everyone would be watching. Marcus didn't care if he finished first. He just wanted to finish. He wanted to prove to himself and everyone else that he was ready. "You can do it, Marcus!" he heard his friends screaming from the roaring bleachers.

At the sound of the horn, Marcus took off running. Speeding around the track, he passed his opponents. Seconds later, he crossed the finish line in third place. Shouts of triumph rang in his ears. He had done it!

Write a story about someone like Marcus who overcame a challenge. How did the person accomplish her feat? The story can be real or imaginary. Use dialogue and descriptive words and phrases to tell your story. After you have finished your first draft, ask a classmate and an adult to read it and give you feedback. Make any necessary changes. Type your final copy.

Prewrite: Use the graphic organizer to plan your story.

Challenge	How the Challenge Was Solved

☀ Reflect and Revise

1. What lessons can we learn from challenges we face?

2. Reread your story. Have you used verb tenses correctly? Are there any inappropriate shifts in verb tense? If so, make any necessary corrections.

Turning Back Time

It was Friday night, and Erica sat at the kitchen table in misery while her friends were on their way to the movies. Erica wanted to go, but she was grounded. Last week, Erica had told her mother that she was going to Ebony's house to study, but instead, they rode the bus to the mall. When Erica's mother found out, she was angry and disappointed.

"First of all, you're too young to go to the mall by yourselves," her mother explained. "Second of all, I trusted you, and I'm not sure I'll be able to trust you again."

As Erica sat at the table, she regretted lying to her mother. Erica wished she could go back in time to last week and start that day over. She would never have been dishonest.

Have you ever wished you could go back in time to a particular day? Was it a good day that you would like to enjoy all over again? Or, was it a bad day that you wish you could change? Write about a day that you wish you could revisit. What would you do differently and why?

Prewrite: Use the graphic organizer to brainstorm ideas for your story.

Beginning

Middle

End

Reflect and Revise

1. Why is it important to reflect on the events in our lives and consider things we might change?

2. Reread your story. Are there a variety of sentence structures? Revise your story to make sure you have included simple, compound, and complex sentences.

Mystery Time

The anticipation of reading mysteries can be scary, funny, and thrilling. The excitement you feel as you read, waiting to get to the end to discover the truth, is priceless. Or, maybe you're a supersleuth who uses your detective skills to solve the mystery before you even reach the end. Read a couple of mysteries to get ideas of how authors grab your attention and develop their stories. How do they keep you interested? Write your own mystery. Introduce the characters and setting of the story. What is the mystery? Who solves it? Do they have any help?

Prewrite: Use the graphic organizer to brainstorm ideas for your story.

Characters			
Mystery to be solved		Solution(s)	
Setting			
Sequence of Events	1.	2.	3.	4.

☀ Reflect and Revise

1. What techniques do mystery authors use to add suspense to their stories? Did you use any of these techniques to add suspense to your story?

2. Reread your story. Have your word choices helped convey the mood you want in the story? If not, consider adding more descriptive or figurative language.

Name _____

Animal Stories

If zoo animals could talk, what do you think they would tell us about their lives? Use multiple sources, including the Internet, magazines, and books, to research zoo animals' routines. Write a story in the first person from the perspective of one zoo animal. Have the animal tell whether he is happy to be safe at the zoo and to know that he will be fed every day. Does your animal feel famous because people visit every day? Does he enjoy people's company, or does he wish people would just go away? Use a clear sequence of events to tell your story. Use descriptive and figurative language.

Prewrite: Use the graphic organizer to plan your story.

Senses (What does your animal see, taste, hear, smell, and feel?)	Sequence of Events
	Beginning
	Middle
	End

Reflect and Revise

1. How do you think zoo and circus animals' lives are similar? How do you think they are different?

2. Reread your story. How have your word choices helped convey the feelings of your chosen zoo animal? If necessary, consider adding more descriptive or figurative language.

Name _____

Tracking Changes

Think about stories you've read where characters change from the beginning of the stories to the end of the stories. Sometimes, they change because of events in their lives, and sometimes they change because they are just getting older and more mature.

How have you changed in the last two years? Do you have more friends? Are you taller now? Do you like different things? Some of the changes we go through may be physical, but some might be based on our interests and activities. Write an essay about how you have changed. Has anyone or anything influenced these changes in you? After you have finished your first draft, ask an adult to read it and give you feedback. Make any necessary changes. Type your final copy.

Prewrite: Use the graphic organizer to record your thoughts.

Then	Now

✺ Reflect and Revise

1. How do you think you will change in the *next* two years? How do you hope to be different? What do you hope will stay the same?

2. Reread your essay. Have you used verb tenses correctly? Are there any inappropriate shifts in verb tense? If so, make any necessary corrections.

Family and Friends

Many of the memories we create are with our families and friends. Brainstorm a list of special times you've had with your family or friends. Choose a memory from the list that you can write about in detail. Was it a special occasion or just an ordinary day? Who was there to share this memory with you? Write a descriptive story about this special memory you had with your family or friends. After you have finished your first draft, ask a classmate and an adult to read it and give you feedback. Make any necessary changes. Type your final copy.

Prewrite: Use the graphic organizer to brainstorm ideas for your story.

Memory	
Setting	
Sights	
Sounds	
First	
Next	
Then	
Finally	

☀ Reflect and Revise

1. Why are memories important in everyone's lives? Why is it important to remember the good things that happen as well as the bad things?

2. Reread your story. Have your word choices helped convey your feelings about the event? Do the readers feel as though they were there? If not, consider adding more descriptive language or using figurative language in your descriptions.

Goals

A major part of being successful is having goals and working hard to meet them. Think about the things you would like to accomplish. What would you like to accomplish as a short-term goal? What would you like to accomplish as a long-term goal? Brainstorm a list of goals. Then, choose one short-term goal and one long-term goal. Do you anticipate any challenges with reaching these goals? If so, how will you prepare for the challenges? Describe how you can hold yourself accountable for meeting these goals. Will you have checkpoints or a buddy system to track your progress? Write a journal entry that describes how you plan to meet these goals and why they are important.

Prewrite: Use the graphic organizer to brainstorm ideas for your journal entry.

Short-term goals	How can I meet these goals?

Long-term goals	How can I meet these goals?

✳ Reflect and Revise

1. Why is it important to set goals? How does it make you feel when you accomplish something you have set out to do?

2. Reread your journal entry. Check for correct capitalization, punctuation, and spelling. Correct any errors.

Transportation Book

Transportation has changed over time, providing easier ways to travel. Work with three or four of your classmates. Create a transportation book that represents transportation over time. Each of you will choose and research a different form of transportation. Include inventors and the time frames. Consider the benefits of your chosen mode of transportation. Use multiple sources, including the Internet and books, to gather information. Cite your sources. Write a report that describes the history of each form of transportation. Once you and your classmates have typed your individual reports, collaborate to compile the transportation book.

Prewrite: Use the graphic organizer to record facts about your chosen mode of transportation.

Mode of Transportation	Fact 1	Fact 2	Fact 3	Fact 4	Fact 5

☀ Reflect and Revise

1. As you and your group members researched the different modes of transportation, you noted the benefits of each. What were some of the drawbacks of each mode of transportation? Think about cost, availability, ease of use, etc.

2. Reread your report. Have you used verb tenses correctly? Are there any inappropriate shifts in verb tense? If so, make any necessary corrections.

Name _____

Family Field Trip

Summer is a great time to learn new things. Your parents have decided that your family will take an educational vacation this summer, and you get to choose the destination. For one week, you will travel to a destination of your choice, but it must be a trip where you will learn about the history of that area and what it has to offer visitors and residents.

Choose a location that you would like to visit and learn more about. Use multiple sources, including the Internet and books, to gather information. Cite your sources. Write a report in which you list and describe places in the area to visit with your family. Explain why each of these locations is important to learning about your chosen destination.

Prewrite: Use the graphic organizer to record information about your vacation destination.

Destination _____				
	Monuments	**Museums**	**Other visitor attractions**	**Other facts/places**
Locations to visit				
Why we should visit				

☀ Reflect and Revise

1. What does the region you live in have to offer? If you had visitors for a week in the summer, where would you take them so that they could learn more about your region?

2. Reread your report. Check for correct capitalization, punctuation, and spelling. Correct any errors.

Around the World

It would be amazing if we could travel to any country in the world. We could explore different cultures, landmarks, and languages. Sometimes, technology allows us to explore without ever leaving our classrooms.

Choose a country in Europe that you would like to learn more about. Use the Internet and books to gather information. Cite your sources. Research the culture, language, and foods. Research the landmarks, population, famous people, etc. Complete a research paper about the country. After you have finished your first draft, ask an adult to read it and give you feedback. Make any necessary changes. Type your final copy. Happy Travels!

Prewrite: Use the graphic organizer to record information about your chosen country.

Country _____   Population _____

Culture	Landmarks	Famous people (artists, musicians, etc.)	Other interesting facts

☀ Reflect and Revise

1. As you researched the European country, what differences did you find between it and the country where you live? Share your findings with a classmate. What differences do you notice between the country you chose to research and the country she chose to research?

2. As you researched the country, did you see words you didn't know? Use context clues to help you understand the words. Use a dictionary if necessary. Use the words and define them in your research paper.

Love Your Organs

Your body has many organs. Organs work together to give your body what it needs to survive. Your lungs are organs that help you breathe. The lungs work with the diaphragm to make breathing comfortable. It's important to have healthy lungs.

Read to learn more about important organs in the body. Choose one organ that you would like to learn more about. Use multiple sources, including the Internet and books, to gather information. Cite your sources. Where is the organ located in the body? What is the function of the organ? Do you need this particular organ to survive? What does it look like? What other organs or body parts help the organ work? Write a report about the organ. Divide your report into sections. Use a heading to introduce each section.

Prewrite: Use the graphic organizer to record information about your chosen organ.

Name of Organ _____			
Location	**Function**	**Description**	**Other organs/body parts that help the organ work**

✺ Reflect and Revise

1. What are some things you can do to take care of your chosen organ? How can you ensure that it stays healthy?

2. As you researched the organ, did you see words you didn't know? Use context clues to help you understand the words. Use a dictionary if necessary. Use the words and define them in your report.

Technology Today

Technology has changed a lot over the years. Many of the digital tools we have today were not available 50 years ago. These tools help us communicate better.

One technology tool is the telephone. Research how the phone has changed since the 1960s. Use the Internet and books to research phones back then and phones now. What are phones able to do now that they weren't able to do then? How have they evolved? Write a report that compares and contrasts the phones from the 1960s with the phones we have today. Include pictures as visual aids with your report. After you have finished your first draft, ask an adult to read it and give you feedback. Make any necessary changes. Type your final copy.

Prewrite: Use the Venn diagram to compare and contrast phones from the 1960s and today. Label each side.

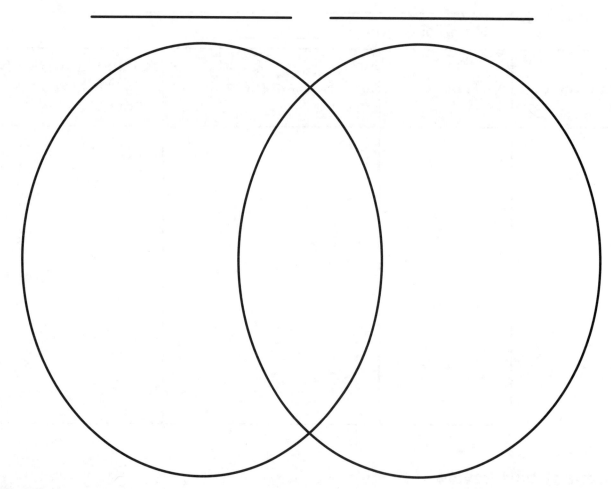

☀ Reflect and Revise

1. How do you imagine phones might be different 20 years from now?

2. Reread your report. Have you used grade-appropriate vocabulary and words that signal you are comparing and contrasting the phones? If not, consider your word choices for clarity (for example, *similarly, in contrast, unlike*).

When I Grow Up

It's never too early to think about what you would like to do when you grow up. It's a good idea to know about different occupations that might interest you.

Brainstorm a list of careers you think you might like to pursue. Choose one career from the list that you would like to learn more about. Use multiple sources, including the Internet, magazines, and books, to research the job. Interview people who have knowledge of the job. What are the responsibilities of the job? How much money might you make doing this job? Can you live anywhere and have this job? Is going to college a requirement for this job? What experience or training do you need? Why do you think you might want this job? Write a report to describe your dream job.

Prewrite: Use the graphic organizer to record your thoughts and findings.

Responsibilities	Income	Location	Required Education	Other Job Requirements

Reflect and Revise

1. Even though being an adult seems a long time away, what are some things you can do now to prepare for your future job? What can you do now to make sure you're on the right track?

2. Reread your report. Have you used verb tenses correctly? Are there any inappropriate shifts in verb tense? If so, make any necessary corrections.

Partner Planets

Planets are amazing places in the solar system. The solar system has inner and outer planets that rotate around the sun. Each of these planets has characteristics that make it different from the others. Some of the planets have rocky surfaces, while some of them have many layers of gas.

With a partner, choose two planets other than Earth to research. Use multiple sources, including the Internet and books, to gather information. How close are the planets to the sun? What is the surface like on each planet? How large are the planets? How long does a day last on each planet? Include other fun facts about the planets. With your partner, write a report that compares and contrasts the two planets. Type your final copy.

Prewrite: Use the graphic organizer to compare and contrast the two planets. Label each side.

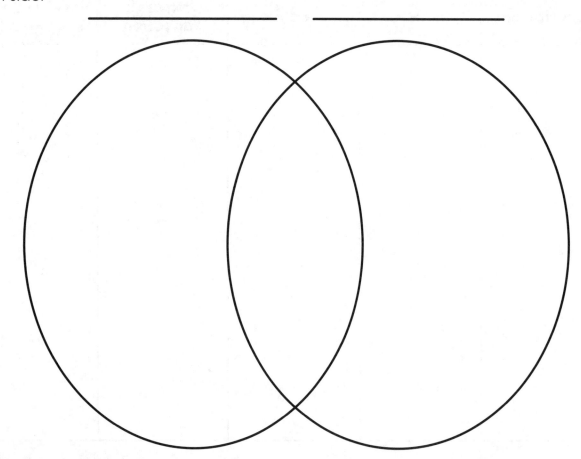

✺ Reflect and Revise

1. Earth is the only planet in our solar system where people live. Based on what you have learned about your two chosen planets, why is it not possible for people to live there?

2. Reread your report. Have you used grade-appropriate vocabulary and words that signal you are comparing and contrasting the planets? If not, consider your word choices for clarity (for example, *similarly, in contrast, unlike*).

Water Conservation

Think of the ways your family consumes water every day. Washing dishes, taking baths or showers, and watering lawns are ways we may use water in our homes. The average family uses 400 gallons (1514 L) of water every day. Less than one percent of Earth's water can be used for these tasks. The rest of the water is salt water or frozen. Therefore, it is important to make sure we don't waste water.

Imagine you have been asked to give a speech to your classmates about the benefits of saving water. Use the Internet and books to gather information. Interview adults to gain some insight about conserving water. Cite your sources. Why is water so important to our lives? How can you save water at home? How can you save water at school? How can you help others save water? Write a speech that shows you understand the importance of conserving water.

Prewrite: Use the graphic organizer to record your thoughts and findings.

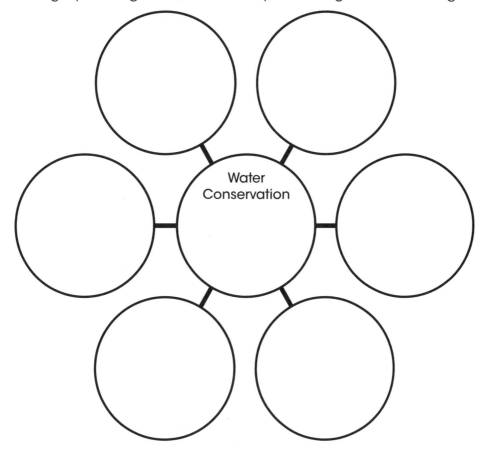

 Reflect and Revise

1. Saving water is important to everyone. How can you make others aware of ways to save water? How can you use this knowledge to make a difference?

2. As you researched water conservation, did you see words you didn't know? Use context clues to help you understand the words. Use a dictionary if necessary. Use the words and define them in your speech.

Name _____

Government Systems

When the founding fathers of the United States created the government system, they did not want any one group or person to have too much power. Therefore, the US Constitution contains a separation of power. Other countries around the world have different government systems.

If you live in the United States, research the branches of government with two classmates. If not, research the government system of your country with two classmates. Use the Internet and books to gather information. What is your government's role? How are representatives chosen? Collaborate with your classmates to write a report about how your government works. Use technology to create a report about how your government works.

Prewrite: Use the graphic organizer to record facts about your government.

Government	Fact 1	Fact 2	Fact 3	Fact 4	Fact 5

Reflect and Revise

1. What are some of your government's strengths?

2. As you researched your government, did you see words you didn't know? Use context clues to help you understand the words. Use a dictionary or other reference materials if necessary. Use the words and define them in your report.

Amazing Amphibians

Amphibians are unique creatures. They are cold-blooded animals that breathe through their skin. Amphibians change a lot from the time they hatch to the time they become adults.

Choose one amphibian that you would like to learn more about. Use multiple sources, including the Internet and books, to gather information. What does the amphibian look like? Where can it be found? What does it eat? How does it change from birth to adult? What other fun facts can you find? As you research, focus on the main ideas and details of the text. Write a report that summarizes what you have learned about the amphibian. Divide your report into sections. Use a heading to introduce each section.

Prewrite: Use the graphic organizer to record information about your chosen amphibian.

Main idea	Details
	• • •
Main idea	**Details**
	• • •
Main idea	**Details**
	• • •

Reflect and Revise

1. How does your chosen amphibian interact with the environment? What are its predators? What is its prey? Does it benefit people? If so, how?

2. As you researched different amphibians, did you see words you didn't know? Use context clues to help you understand the words. Use a dictionary if necessary. Use the words and define them in your report.

Name _____

Wacky Weather

Weather impacts us in many ways. When major storms strike, they often cause damage to homes, businesses, and natural resources.

Imagine your teacher has asked you and a classmate to be the class meteorologists. As meteorologists, you and your classmate will choose two major storms such as tornadoes, tsunamis, or hurricanes to research. You will compare and contrast the two storms. Use multiple sources, including the Internet and books, to gather information. How do these storms form? How long do they last? What are the warning signs? Are some of the storms stronger than others? Where do they occur? What other facts can you find? Use technology to create a report about the two storms.

Prewrite: Use the graphic organizer to compare and contrast the storms. Label each side.

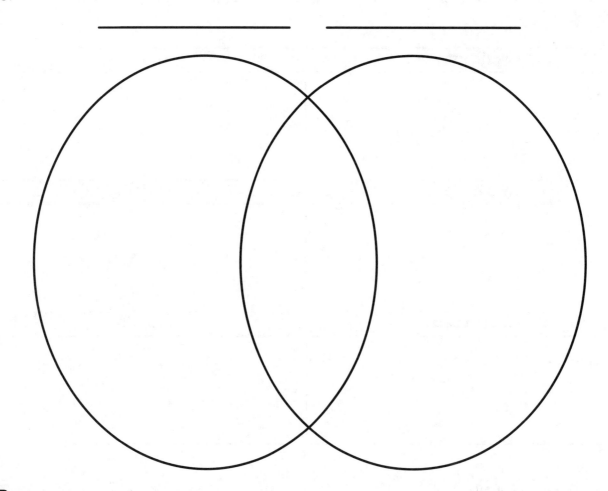

✳ Reflect and Revise

1. How would you tell your classmates to prepare for each storm? What would you suggest for creating a safety plan?

2. Reread your report. Have you used grade-appropriate vocabulary and words that signal you are comparing and contrasting the storms? If not, consider your word choices for clarity (for example, *similarly, in contrast, unlike*).

Save Our Trees

While riding down the street or playing in the park, we may not always notice the trees around us. Nature is an important part of our survival, particularly natural resources such as trees. Often, trees are cut down to build houses or buildings. Many groups work to preserve trees. Why is this important?

Research the benefits of trees. Use multiple resources to gather information, including the Internet, magazines, and books. How do trees help people? How do they help the environment? What organizations support saving trees? Write a report about the benefits of trees. After you have finished your first draft, ask a classmate and an adult to read it and give you feedback. Make any necessary changes. Type your final copy.

Prewrite: Use the graphic organizer to record facts about the benefits of trees.

Benefits of Trees				
Fact 1	Fact 2	Fact 3	Fact 4	Fact 5

Reflect and Revise

1. Often, trees are cut down to make products. How can we reduce the number of trees that are cut down to make products?

2. Reread your report. Check for correct capitalization, punctuation, and spelling. Correct any errors.

Exploring History

Each region of a country has special stories that represent the pride and culture of the people. These stories are often told in historic places. Some of these places are in the form of memorials or museums. Some places are battle locations or heroes' homes.

Research historic sites in your region using books, magazines, or the Internet. Choose a site that you would like to learn more about. What is the historical significance of this site? When did it become a historic site, and where is it located? What would you learn if you visited this site? What other people might enjoy visiting this site? What groups of people or individuals are associated with this site? Why is it important to learn about this site? How does this site represent your region? Write a report that summarizes what you have learned about this historic site.

Prewrite: Use the graphic organizer to record facts about your chosen historic site.

> Introduction

Fact 1 _____ Fact 2 _____

Fact 3 _____ Fact 4 _____

Fact 5 _____ Fact 6 _____

Fact 7 _____ Fact 8 _____

> Conclusion

Reflect and Revise

1. What is the purpose of having historic sites? Do they benefit the community? Why or why not?

2. Reread your report. Check for correct capitalization, punctuation, and spelling. Correct any errors.

Name _____

Amazing Animals

Elephants are intriguing animals. They are the largest mammals that live on land. Elephants have long trunks that help them smell, eat, and drink. Their ivory tusks help them dig, gather food, and defend themselves. These land animals have many characteristics that make them unique.

Choose a land animal that you would like to learn more about. Use multiple sources to gather information, including the Internet, magazines, and books. Where does the animal live? What does it eat? How much does it weigh? How would you describe the physical characteristics of the animal? What other fun facts can you find? Write a report that summarizes what you have learned about the animal. Divide your report into sections. Use a heading to introduce each section. After you have finished your first draft, ask an adult to read it and give you feedback. Make any necessary changes.

Prewrite: Use the graphic organizer to record facts about your chosen animal.

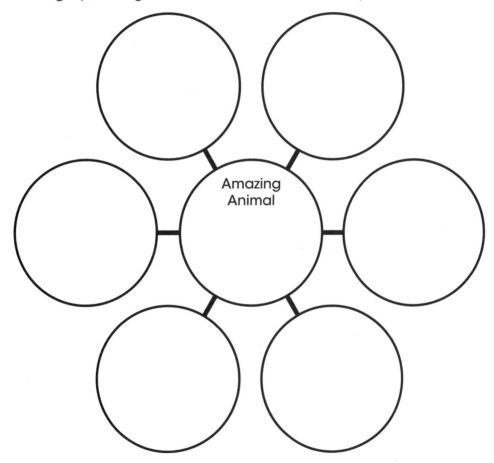

Amazing Animal

☀ Reflect and Revise

1. How is your chosen animal different from other land animals? What are some things the animal has in common with other land animals?

2. Reread your report. Check for correct capitalization, punctuation, and spelling. Correct any errors.

Answer Key

Because writing is personal and presentations are unique, there are no "correct answers" to be applied to students' work. However, students should follow the instruction of the writing prompts, fill in the graphic organizers, and apply the steps of the writing process. Use the guidelines below or the Writing Rubric on page 4 to help you assess students' work.

Pages 6 to 10: Writing Practice Packet

Check students' work throughout the writing process practice pages. Help students master each step before going on to another. Use this process with other writing prompts if more practice is needed before independent writing begins. Refer students to these pages as needed.

Pages 11 to 63: Reflect and Revise

These sections, at the end of each writing prompt page, ask students first to reflect and to consider alternative or additional slants to their topics. Often, it is requested that they add this additional layer of thought to their writing. Assess accordingly: First, check that students have fulfilled the challenge; second, check that they have applied their conclusions to the writing if asked. Because the Common Core language standards are tied so tightly to the writing standards, the second halves of these sections address various standards. Check through written work for mastery.

Pages 11 to 23: Opinion/Argumentative Writing

Check graphic organizers. Essays, reports, and letters will vary, but opinions should be supported with reasons and show evidence based on research, interviews, or recollection of experiences. Look for application of critical thinking and personal reflection. Each writing product should have an organized structure with a clear introduction, body, and conclusion.

Pages 24 to 36: Informative/Explanatory Writing

Check graphic organizers. Reports will vary but should be based on research or interviews. Look for an emphasis on facts and concrete details. Facts should be grouped in paragraphs according to topic. Information should be presented using the structure of an introduction, body, and conclusion. Look for content-specific vocabulary used to expand on the topic. If not evident, encourage students to connect ideas with linking words and phrases.

Pages 37 to 49: Narrative Writing

Check graphic organizers. Stories, essays, and other narrative formats will vary but should respond to all items in the prompt. Look for clear and logical sequences of events and a variety of transitional words and phrases. Students should use descriptive or figurative language to clearly convey experiences. Stories should include a narrator and/or characters and provide setting details.

Pages 50 to 63: Research Writing

Check graphic organizers. Reports will vary but should be based on research or interviews. Assess students' abilities to examine topics and convey ideas and information clearly to their readers. Look for an emphasis on facts and concrete details. Students should use logical organizational structures, including introductory and concluding paragraphs.